The Little

Sleep

Paul Wilson

Secrets for a blissful sleep
by the bestselling author of
The Little Book of Calm

BARNES
&NOBLE
BOOKS
NEW YORK

*R*emember how wonderful it felt to awaken —
refreshed, alive, eager to make the most of the day?
With no recollection of the preceding eight hours
except that it was deep, satisfying, undisturbed slumber?

Every morning could be like that.

Remember how your dreams could excite you, even days
after the event? And those all-too-rare moments of bliss as
you drifted off to sleep, your consciousness floating
between illumination and tranquillity?

You can recapture those feelings tonight.

The Little Book of Sleep was created to add beauty to
your slumber.

Page after page of inspirations and suggestions to
enrich your rest, and make bedtime one of the highlights of
your day.

Let this book fall open to any page for the suggestion
that will work best for you tonight. Accept it at face value.
Let your subconscious have its way. Then, lie back and
enjoy it.

Oh, yes . . . and pleasant dreams!

Take rest

Take rest; a field that has rested gives
a beautiful crop.

—Ovid

No time for the nightcap

There is a widespread belief that the sedating properties of alcohol will assist your sleep. Not so. In fact, the opposite is usually the case: while alcohol may sometimes invite sleep, it usually disrupts the rest of your night by also inviting restlessness and early morning awakening.

Peace comes through the window

Fresh air is one of the cheapest aids to a deep, satisfying rest. The more oxygen you imbibe, the more physically relaxed you will feel.

Leave the window open a little, even in cool weather, and allow sleep to breeze in, in the most wholesome way.

Cover yourself

As a baby you were conditioned to believe
that sound sleep and cozy bedcovers
went together.

You can take advantage of that conditioning
and recapture that childlike sense of security
by always using a light cover when you sleep.
Even in warm weather, it works.

Give thanks to cows

Old wives have been telling us this since
Adam was a baby, but milk really does work
as a soothing late night drink. Because it con-
tains calcium and the amino acid tryptophan —
both of which help the body to relax — milk
is a natural aid to sleep.

Make your coffee

Coffee and, to a lesser extent, tea were purposely designed to stimulate, to wake you up. Even small quantities will have an effect on your sleep — the caffeine can remain in your system for six to twelve hours, sometimes longer.

For the sake of an untroubled rest, consider avoiding coffee altogether in the afternoons and evenings.

Press on the cool

You can add a degree of sensuality to your rest, and press away the tensions of the day at the same time, with a simple silk eyepress.

Fill a small silk bag with lentils or linseeds, place it over your closed eyes, and feel the gentle relaxation envelop your entire body.

Nature's tranquilizer

Valerian is known as Nature's tranquilizer. It is a restorative relaxant, classified as a nervine, a herb that helps to reduce tension in your nervous system.

Whether taken in tablet, tincture or tea, valerian can be most effective in transforming restlessness into a peaceful rest — without the drowsy hangover effect produced by many chemical sedatives.

Lie back and enjoy it

There will be times when sleep is not
meant to happen.

On such occasions you have a choice: either
lose sleep over losing sleep, or appreciate
the sheer luxury of having nothing to do and a
few hours of peace in which to do it.

Take the easy way out and treat those
moments as an indulgence. Rest easy in the
knowledge that, even if you're not sleeping,
you're still getting valuable rest.

Celebrate the day

When was the last time you were treated to breakfast in bed? To build the association between feeling relaxed and being in bed, indulge yourself with this little luxury from time to time.

Meditate early

Although meditation will work wonders in helping you to rest better, you may discover that doing it just before you retire can have a rousing effect.

The ideal times for meditation are the times when you want to feel refreshed and awake: early mornings and early evenings. Meditate then and you'll sleep like a baby at night.

Relish the act of creation

The moments of your day when you are
most creative, are those moments just before
you fall asleep.

According to Arthur Koestler, "The most
fertile region [in the mind's inner landscape]
seems to be the marshy shore between
sleep and full awakening."

Relax and enjoy it.

Say cheese in the sun

A good level of calcium in the diet helps to overcome sleeplessness.

Not only will you find calcium in dairy products such as cheese, but in green leafy vegetables, almonds, tofu and some fish. For the calcium to be effectively metabolized by the body, you also need vitamin D which is absorbed through the skin from sunlight. (Coffee and alcohol inhibit its effectiveness.)

Dream of sleep

Whenever you feel that sleep will never come,
conjure a picture of yourself dreaming.
Imagine what you look like in that state, how
you sound, what the bed feels like beneath
you. Chances are, you'll soon become part of
that dream. Make it a happy one.

Pretend it's the Thirties

Remember the beautiful silk pyjamas the Hollywood movie goddesses used to wear in the Thirties? How could you fail to sleep beautifully in pyjamas like those?

Indulge yourself with quality silk worn next to your bare flesh, and your bedtime will take on a pleasurable dimension you may never have considered.

Soak before sleep

A leisurely warm bath before bedtime dissolves all the day's tension from your muscles and gently puts you in the mood for sleep. Surprisingly, this practice is even more relaxing on those occasions you would least expect it — in warm weather. Add a few drops of lavender and marjoram oils, and the rest will be all the more tranquil.

Make love

Nothing releases tension, takes your mind off the day-to-day, and prepares you for tomorrow like making love. Make it with someone you love, and the contented feelings that follow will make your sleep even more satisfying.

Throw off a blanket

It's hard to imagine sleep without blankets. While the ideal is to be warm, and to be covered, the heavier your covers, the lighter your sleep.

"Just right" normally brings a sounder and more pleasant sleep than "warm as toast".

Drop on your pillow

A couple of drops of marjoram or lavender oils, or your favorite relaxing essential oil, will not only encourage sleep, but pleasant dreams as well. Drop the oil onto a handkerchief and slip it inside your pillow case.

No news is good news

Getting lost in an involving, or even a boring book can be a great way to unwind in the moments before sleep. Newspapers and news magazines, on the other hand, can have the opposite effect. These publications are invariably filled with gloom and negative reports — not the sort of stuff you want coloring your thoughts and feelings in the fading moments of the day.

Snuggle

You can double the coziness and satisfaction of your sleep simply by snuggling up to a friendly body.

The contentedness that flows from this should make you feel like sleeping.

Get it off your chest

There is nothing like a clear conscience to
clear the way for an untroubled rest.

Invest in mattress real estate

You are more intimate with your mattress,
and spend much more time with it, than
any other piece of furniture.
Invest in your mattress: the bigger
and firmer your mattress, the more luxurious
your sleep.

Wake when you're told to

You can live without an alarm clock. If you simply tell yourself "Tomorrow I will wake at 7:00 A.M.", you will wake at 7:00 A.M. As long as you trust your subconscious and don't keep checking the clock throughout the night, you will wake on the dot. Every time.

Mull up some mulberry

Here is a recipe for a fruity tranquilizer I found in an old book on Chinese medicine: boil a kilogram of fresh mulberries in water. After thirty minutes, pour out the water, add more, and boil again. After thirty minutes add back the original liquid, and reduce it to a sticky concoction to which you add honey, and continue to boil for two more minutes.

Take one teaspoonful of this mixture, twice daily, to help you sleep.

Don't lose sleep over not sleeping

One of the peculiarities of being wide awake in bed is that it often induces anxiety of its own.

If you can view life as an adventure — where you can never accurately predict the outcome — then being awake simply becomes part of that adventure. Who knows where it will lead? Who knows what you will discover about yourself in the tranquil moments of half sleep.

Sleep with a chamomile

Chamomile is one of nature's gentlest and
most effective relaxants. It is readily available
as a tea which you can modify to your taste
with honey and lemon. Equally as relaxing, add
a few drops of chamomile oil to your bath
before bedtime.

Think of feet

If you have trouble relaxing at night, concentrate on relaxing your feet. Think of their texture and weight. Using only your thoughts, try to relax them. When you feel them relax, gradually work this relaxing feeling up your legs, to your thighs, your buttocks, your lower back, your back . . . until your whole body is relaxed.

Concentrate on relaxing; let sleep take care of itself.

Become a toddler

Have you ever noticed how small children sleep? They drift off as though they don't have a care in the world, and that their every possible need will be taken care of.

Dwell on this feeling when you retire at night: pretend to yourself that you don't have a care in the world, and that your every need will be taken care of. Then you can sleep like a child too.

Watch out for MSG

Although this becomes less of a problem as we become more aware of dietary issues, the old flavor enhancer, Monosodium glutamate is still used in many restaurants.

MSG can wreak havoc on your sleep. Avoid it at all costs — if for no other reason than good taste.

Sleep natural

You may find that synthetic or heavily colored materials interfere with your body's ability to breathe and for your ability to relax properly. Not only does this apply to your daywear, but to your sleepwear as well.

If you want to enjoy the kind of natural slumber that some people will only ever dream about, begin with natural fibers for your bedclothes and bedcovers.

Soothe yourself to sleep

If you are inclined to restlessness while you are asleep, you will get more than pleasure out of this sensuous, pre-bedtime exercise: mix a few drops of blue chamomile, lavender and neroli oils together (in an almond oil base), and slowly work into your face, neck, and arms — lightly covering every part of your body until you are blissfully relaxed.

Try B3

Many people who suffer from insomnia find that Vitamin B3 (niacin) helps bring on sleep. Both Vitamin B3 and B6 help convert an amino acid, l-tryptophan, into the hormone that helps you to sleep, serotonin. You'll find both of these vitamins in bananas, corn, brown rice, soybeans, wheatbran, brewers yeast, peanuts and meats.

Make them part of your everyday diet — not something you eat just before bedtime, where they can have a rousing effect.

Know when to give in

It's quite natural for all human beings to have
disturbed sleep at certain times of the month
or at certain ages. When these occasions
arise, it's important to recognize that there's
little to be gained in struggling for sleep.
These are the occasions to give in gracefully,
get out of bed and savor the stillness
of the night.

Take an author to bed

Most authors would like their novel to be a rousing, thought-provoking experience. Yet, most people find a good story is a great way to relax and unwind. Especially in bed.

There is a physiological reason for this: as you lose yourself in the reading of a book, you progressively ease into a relaxed, trance-like state. Then, if you give in and go with the flow, sleep should only be a few pages away.

Sleep on your food

Both overeating and undereating disturb
your sleep.

Eat too much, and your metabolism is
quickened and your digestive system has to
work harder, causing you to toss and turn
through the night. Eat too little and hunger
interferes with your rest.

Snack on calming foods such as oatmeal,
whole-wheat bread, cottage cheese, even
turkey and chicken, and you'll sleep
a whole lot better.

Surf

It has long been celebrated that sailors (and surfers and divers) sleep more soundly than landlubbers.

There's a lesson to learned here: if you want to assure yourself of a blissful, deep sleep, spend time in, on, near, or beneath the waves.

Knit one, pearl two

I sometimes think that knitting was designed
as a productive form of meditation. The
repetitive nature of the needles and
patterns are hypnotic in their action, and soon
lull you into to a deeply relaxed state. From
this state, you can move on to sleep, or you
can wake — the choice is yours.

Love lavender

The lavender flower is one of nature's most seductive relaxants. In days past, lavender water was a widely-used scent and relaxant. Even Keats recognized its charm in his poem, The Eve of St. Agnes:

And still she slept an azure-lidded sleep,
In blanched linen, smooth, and lavendered.

Give your foot the knuckle

The sole of the foot is the source of dozens of acupressure points that relate to how relaxed you feel.

To ease yourself into a deeply relaxed state, take your left foot in your left hand and, with the knuckles of your right hand, gently rock backwards and forwards between arch and ball.

This simple pressure will relax the whole body.

*L*isten for the rain

Have you ever gone to bed listening to sound
of the rain on a tin roof?

Just a few minutes of that monotonous
drumming will lure you into the deepest state
of relaxation. Some even find it romantic.

To recreate this relaxing sensation when
the weather is fine, close your eyes and try
recalling that sound.

Grow old gracefully

As you get older, you may sometimes experience a return to the sleep patterns of early childhood: napping during the day, as well as at night.

While this may mean you require less sleep at night, it is entirely natural — something neither to resist, nor to be alarmed about.

Make the most of daytime rests when they occur, and enjoy whatever the night has to offer.

Explore the subtleties of foreign cinema

One of the unsung attractions of the more "subtle" foreign films is their ability to start you yawning. Such films, or indeed any cultural activity that affects you this way, may have much to offer in your search for a way of producing sleep.

Fantasize

When you go to bed tonight, treat yourself to a fantasy.

Maybe you're lying on a sun-bleached tropical island. You can see a solitary cloud floating through the sky above, and can hear the quiet lapping of waves on the shore. You can feel the sand beneath your back and the warmth of the sun on your face. Fantasize that you're drifting off, drifting off . . .

Try sleeping with rose

If you believe in the soothing and healing power of crystals, sleep with a Rose Quartz "Love Stone" under your pillow.

Scientists agree that crystals such as Rose Quartz do have unique physical properties; believers agree that they have the power to remove pressure and to relax the mind.

Sleep quietly

Sleep quietly,
now that
the gates of the day
are closed. Leave tomorrow's
problems for tomorrow.

The earth is peaceful.
Only the starts are abroad;
and they will not
cause you any trouble.

"Sleep," by Max Ehrmann

Have chocolate for breakfast

For some, life would be unbearable without chocolate. Others feel the same about cola.

If you must have stimulants such as chocolate, cola, or coffee, have them before lunch. Even smaller amounts later in the day can produce restlessness at night.

Take the passion to bed

The exotic sounding passion flower, or passiflora, has been used as a sedative for centuries. It works as a calming agent on the nervous system.

You will find passion flower, along with other relaxing herbs — such as hops, skullcap, lemon balm, and limeflower — in teas in your health food store. You'll also find it mixed with chamomile, catnip and valerian in many herbal prescriptions.

Chill your pillow

There is nothing more relaxing and conducive towards rest than a cool, cotton pillow-case on a warm summer's evening.

On really warm nights, try leaving your pillowcase in the refrigerator for a few minutes before retiring. It will help lower the body temperature, which helps bring on sleep.

Breakfast at night

More than most other foodstuffs, humble oats are known for their calming as well as their nutritional properties.

A plate of porridge with milk, therefore, can be the ideal pre-bedtime snack. (You might have difficulty explaining this to your house guests, though.)

Give or take an hour

Some people feel cheated if they miss an hour or two of sleep at night.

However, studies show that six or seven hours of sound sleep will leave you feeling significantly more rested in the morning than eight or nine hours of tossing and turning.

With sleep, quality outweighs quantity every time. So don't feel short changed if you miss an hour or two.

Shrug off loneliness

The stillness of the night exaggerates
loneliness.

The antidote to loneliness is to become
comfortable with, and to enjoy the pleasure of,
your own company. This may seem like an
effort but, once you have mastered this subtle
shift of attitude, you may discover what good
company you can be.

Turn to your brain

One of the functions of the brain is to produce melatonin, a neurochemical that helps to lower your body temperature and induce sleepiness.

Now, in many countries, melatonin can be bought without prescription as an aid to sleep and as an aid to moderate jet lag. But, as with all artificial sleep-inducers, even so-called natural ones, professional advice should be sought before you begin taking any medication.

Let dawn send you to sleep

How many poor sleepers do you know who are early risers? Not many.

While you may discover something refreshing and invigorating about being up before the sun rises, the real appeal of early rising is that it encourages sleep at the end of the day — and that makes rising early *tomorrow* morning even more appealing.

Shift forwards

When you work involves shift work, the best way of maintaining a degree of harmony and comfort in your sleep patterns is to follow the clock forwards.

Next time you change your shift hours, change them clockwise rather than counter-clockwise. Do this and your sleep patterns will adjust to the change more harmoniously.

The good oil on sleep

"Alternative" people have long believed that
essential oils such as lavender, marjoram and
neroli possess powerful calming properties.
Now there is scientific evidence that this is
so: the aromas of oils such as these aid the
production of serotonin, the chemical that
helps you sleep.

Use them in a massage base, or in a
ceramic burner, or add a few drops to your
bath, and discover just how relaxing they
can be.

Pretend you're Mediterranean

There is a belief that the siesta relates more to late lunches and warm weather than to rest cycles. However, the human rest cycle usually occurs twice a day and, yes, the other time is the early afternoon.

If you find that a "normal" nighttime sleep cycle eludes you, or you're searching for a way to get your sleep cycles back into sync, consider this sensible Latin habit.

Rise at six forty-five

Regardless of what hour you get to bed at night, make a practice of waking at the same time every day. The more habitual your rising time becomes, the more habitual your falling asleep time becomes.

Make rest a ritual

Similarly, the more ritualized your bedtime,
the more patterns you establish, the more
you condition yourself to falling asleep at a
specific time of the evening. Make a routine
of bedtime, and you make a routine of sleep.

Catnap on occasions

There will be times when sleep escapes you.
At such times you have a choice: either rail
against wakefulness and suffer the unrest,
or accept what has been dealt, and make up
for it tomorrow.

If you choose the latter, you can get by with
brief catnaps during the day.

As long as you accept that this may be
disruptive to your nighttime rest, it can make
your days more bearable.

Avoid catnaps

If you want to make a routine of restful sleep,
sleep only at night.

That means avoiding catnaps during the day
at all cost — regardless of how much sleep
you have lost in the previous evening. Catnaps
during the day will often extract a price from
your sleep at night. The choice is yours.

The best cure for insomnia
is to get lots of sleep.

—W. C. Fields

Sink and sleep

An entertaining way of forgetting about sleep-lessness is to concentrate on all the external sensations of your body.

Feel the air on your face, your head on the pillow. Feel your skin against the bedclothes. When you can feel the entire length of your body slowly sinking into your mattress, just a fraction of a centimeter, you will be well on the way to sinking into oblivion.

Become well read

Some of the best-read people I've met have difficulty sleeping at night. They have time to indulge their passion.

At the risk of appearing defeatist, if you do have to endure periods of sleeplessness (and it happens to most of us at different phases of life), celebrate the fact that you've found the solution to one of life's most common complaints: "I don't have the time".

Use that time to become well read.

Take French lessons

Several of the French composers from the
late Romantic and early Impressionist eras
made an art of relaxing, entrancing music.
Indulge yourself with the compositions of
Debussy, Fauré, Bizet and Satie — not only to
ease you into a relaxed state, but to fill your
night and soul with beauty.

Rest by the sea

Ever noticed how soundly you sleep when you're within earshot of the surf?

There is more to this than the freshness of the sea air: the rhythm of the ebb and flow of waves is almost identical to the rhythm of the breathing of a deeply relaxed person. The relaxing, repetitive sounds of the ocean waves help most people to float off to into a deep, delta sleep.

Even if you can't live by the sea, you can enjoy the same calming effect by listening to a recording of the ocean waves.

Postpone your worries

The worst part about worries is the way they visit, and appear their bleakest, in the quiet moments of night.

With a minimum of effort you can postpone them until your waking hours — invariably, they will seem less threatening then. Write them down, assuring yourself that you will grant them your full attention the following day. Most will be reduced, if not solved, by morning.

Go to sleep in fashion

As much as bright colors and wispy curtains may please your decorating aesthetics, they are not always conducive to sound sleep. Dark bedrooms, or at the very minimum, light proof curtains, are your starting point for an uninterrupted rest.

Hide the clock

The presence of a clock in your bedroom can be a constant reminder of any sleep you may be missing out on. Its very presence is often all that's necessary to keep your mind ticking away when it should be at rest.

Leave your clock outside, and you have a better chance of finding sleep inside.

Think ahead

Rational people become irrational when they're denied sleep, and small problems become giant ones. A powerful way to reduce the size of problems is to use your imagination. Imagine yourself in ten years' time: imagine what you'll be wearing, where you'll be living, how you'll be feeling. Then try to imagine how you will feel then about the problems you're wrestling with now.

Nine times out of ten they'll diminish.

Spring clean

If all else fails, and sleep is never going to arrive, get out of bed and start doing something menial and boring — like spring cleaning, or filing. Be meticulous; do it to the best of your ability; and, most importantly, keep going until you have completed the chores you set yourself.

Two or three nights is all it takes to cure the most persistent insomnia.

Sleep comes quickly when your subconscious knows the alternative is sitting up polishing the silver.

Keep a *journal*

Journal writing has much to offer those who
have trouble sleeping. It helps you to put
problems into perspective. It is a record of
your sleep habits. And, over and above all
else, it is a quiet, reflective activity that often
induces a languor of its own.

Have a *three hour famine*

If you want to sleep easily and sleep soundly,
the time to complete dinner is three hours
before bedtime. Providing you don't go to bed
feeling hungry, the earlier you eat, the better
you sleep.

Escape the light

Any form of light can inhibit the production of the protein you require to produce melatonin, the body's most important sleep-producing hormone. Remove all lights from your bedroom, even the LED glow on your alarm clock, and you'll sleep better.

Be aware of six things

Focus on one bright spot then, with your peripheral vision, note six different things you can see. Without allowing your eyes to stray, note six different sounds you can hear. Then six things you can feel.

Next, note only five. Then four, three, two, one . . .

If you're ever going to fall asleep, you will be asleep by one . . .

Look forward to the dream time

When you cease to dream you cease to live.

—Malcolm S. Forbes

Switch off the EMFs

Electromagnetic fields (EMFs) created by electric current or appliances may influence your dominant brain wave states — particularly those you depend on for a good night's sleep.

The worst offender is the clock radio, followed by the television set or video recorder on standby, and sometimes even your electric blanket. Banishing these from your bedroom often banishes some of the great obstacles to sleep.

Forgive

How often do you find sleep is interrupted
or prevented by the ill-feelings you carry
towards others?

There is no reason for you to trouble yourself this way. If you find yourself bothered by
these feelings, you have two choices: either
work out the problem, or forgive completely.
It will leave you feeling much more at peace.

The good oil on jet lag

A pleasant way around jet lag is by using essential oils.

If you arrive at your destination during the day, immediately make yourself a warm bath with a few drops of rosemary and sandalwood. After a leisurely soak, go about your business for the day.

If you arrive at night, use lavender and sandalwood, perhaps with a little ylang ylang. Then slip into bed and into your destination's sleep zone.

Turn off the power

A falling body temperature is the body's way of helping you to fall asleep. Hence, as appealing it may seem on a chilly night, an electric blanket can interfere with your rest if left turned on.

For the most luxurious repose, use your electric blanket to warm the bed *before* bedtime — then turn it off before you retire.

Sleep on a sheep

As any baby will tell you, a sheepskin under-blanket really stands out from the flock when it comes to encouraging the deepest sleep.

This is not just because of the physical sensation. There is a unique property of wool that allows your body to perspire in vapor form rather than liquid, and this contributes to a more relaxed, natural-feeling sleep.

Learn to hover

Astral travel is not for everybody. But believers and participants insist it always happens in the deepest of sleeps.

You can emulate this experience by imagining your body floating a fraction of a centimeter above the bed. When you can really sense what this feels like, when you can sense the space between you and the bed, you will have put aside all thoughts of the "here and now" and who knows where you might be headed.

Wait for the wearies

All people are different: most get tired around
ten, some earlier. Others are still not tired
at midnight.

You can make a habit of turning tiredness into
sleep simply by waiting until you're drowsy
before going to bed.

Study your pillow

One pillow could be all that stands between you and a beautiful sleep.

With so many different pillow types on offer today, you can almost certainly find the one that suits your anatomy and temperament. Experiment. You'll probably end up wondering why you've never wondered about this before.

Convince yourself you've been sleeping

Take comfort in the fact that studies show
many people who claim to be insomniac are
either normal sleepers, or lose less than
thirty minutes of sleep a night. Moreover,
most of them are asleep within twenty minutes
of placing their heads on the pillow.

Often the belief you're not getting sleep
is no more than that — a belief.

Leave work for work

Hard-working people often have sleep problems because they don't know how to stop working after going to bed.

Make a ritual of stopping work at a specific time each day. Choose a cutoff place, time, or event that signals the end of your working day. Make a list of things that should be resumed the following day, then retire for the night with a clear mind.

Get negative

Ever noticed that you sleep extra soundly
when you're near the sea or after a thunder-
storm has passed?

It's because of the negative ions in the
atmosphere.

A low-cost negative ion generator, or ionizer,
is an electronic way of producing these relaxing, mood-enhancing particles. Sleep with one
beside your bed — especially if you're in an
air-conditioned or centrally heated room —
and you'll find many positives in negative ions.

Light up your fingers

When you're in bed tonight, imagine a lightness in the tips of your fingers. Keep your hands still by your side, and imagine this lightness almost lifting your fingers from your bed. Now imagine the same lightness in your toes. Feel it lifting upwards.

If ten minutes of this doesn't send you to sleep, it will certainly have you feeling deeply relaxed, and you know where that leads . . .

Plug in the quiet

There is a simple, cheap antidote to noisy neighbors or neighborhoods: soft ear plugs.

A pleasing alternative is to play soft, relaxing music through headphones. And, if you use the same music each time you do this, you begin to create a calming association with that particular piece — then you'll find it works all the more quickly.

Design an angst stretch

Anger can be a major cause of sleep
interruption.

It is not always easy to forgive or forget,
and may sometimes seem impossible to work
through the cause of your anger. A more
creative alternative is to choose one time and
place each day to vent your negative feelings.
Do it on your daily walk, for example, on a
designated "angst stretch" — where you
exercise your hostile feelings, then
abandon them until next time. Then approach
bedtime in a positive frame of mind.

Escape outdoors

You will have noticed how spent you feel after spending time in the clean mountain air, or the refreshing sea breeze, or in the wide open spaces. Outdoor places such as these not only help you to feel that you've spent the day well, but also help you to sleep more soundly at night.

Spend time outdoors for a better sleep indoors.

Recall your last facial

Remember how peaceful you felt, how you drifted off into a halcyon state the last time you had a facial?

You can clone that experience in bed tonight, bringing back that deep sense of relaxation, simply by applying a warm, wet face-towel, scented with a few drops of lavender oil.

Turn on the hum

Travelers on submarines and ocean cruisers
soon make an amazing discovery about the
nature of sound: you sleep soundly while
engines are running only to wake when
they stop.

The low-pitched hum produced by engines
and some air-conditioners often occurs at the
same frequency that the brain produces, and
locks into, in delta sleep.

Instruct yourself to sleep

Often when you have difficulty sleeping, the words that play through your thoughts exacerbate the condition. Unspoken instructions like, "I'll never get to sleep if this continues," tend to become self-fulfilling.

Better to issue new (unspoken) instructions for your thoughts, like: "If I lie here and relax, and listen to my breathing, sleep will soon be here".

Light up and stay up

This probably won't make it easier for you to give up smoking, but it is worth recognizing that nicotine is a stimulant. A stimulant that disturbs sleep.

If you are committed to being a smoker, yet you want to sleep soundly, avoid cigarettes for at least two hours before bedtime.

Lessen the tension

Women who suffer from PMS know how disruptive this can be to their sleep patterns.

While the ubiquitous Evening Primrose Oil does assist, there is another remedy that many believe is even more powerful: St. John's Wort (hypericum). Its calming and sedative properties help induce sleep without producing drowsiness the following day.

Pray for sleep

There is a psychological benefit from prayer that is often overlooked in the spirituality that accompanies it. Within the brain is a place sometimes referred to as "the God spot". Accessing this place mentally will produce feelings of peace and transcendence.

Those who pray, and derive comfort and satisfaction from the activity, and are seldom left feeling sleep deprived.

Down the wild jujube

There is a range of herbs in Chinese medicine used to treat sleep problems — Wild Jujube, Lotus seed, and many more.

You might never have these prescribed, however, because traditional Chinese herbalists eschew simplistic diagnoses such as "insomnia", and may search for more relevant underlying conditions.

If you have a chronic sleep disorder, Chinese herbalism could work for you.

Get fresh with your sheets

What is it about crisp, fresh linen makes you want to drift off the moment you slip between the covers?

Whether it's the simple, physical sensation of that freshly laundered surface, or the thought of approaching the night untainted by the past, it is an experience that's worth exploring on a regular basis. Use fresh sheets as often as your laundry will allow.

Choose between sleep and vampires

For hundreds of years, garlic has been one of the favored safeguards against vampire attacks at night. Perhaps the way it works is in preventing you from sleeping too deeply.

As some yogis will tell you, excessive garlic, salt, and spices induce restlessness. Too much late at night is a recipe for unrest. Eat earlier, or choose more calming foods before bedtime.

Get out of the house

Melatonin is the hormone that makes your body want to sleep. Sunlight (which produces melanin) encourages the body to readily produce this hormone.

If illness or disability confines you to the house, try to submit yourself to a little sunshine as often as you can. It may help you to sleep better.

Turn the room blue

Colors, like sounds, not only have an impact on your emotions, but on your physiology as well. The wavelengths of colors such as blue and green, or pastel pink, encourage restful feelings — whereas the more dynamic primary colors stimulate.

Paint your bedroom in restful colors and you'll find sleep comes much easier.

Start at the temple

One of the most relaxing acupressure points on the body is one you intuitively reach for when you're under pressure — at your temples.

Massage your temples in a light circular motion, then stroke your forehead from your eyebrows past the temples, and you'll stroke yourself into a deeper and deeper state of relaxation.

Expect nothing

One of the most comforting pieces of advice
ever offered by an old Zen master was this:
expect nothing. Sometimes sleep is good,
sometimes it is merely OK, sometimes you
miss out altogether. This is the way of life.
Expect nothing, and you'll enjoy whatever
arrives all the more.

Practice solitaire

The card game, solitaire, was designed to send you to sleep. Undemanding, repetitive, requiring concentration but little mental effort, it will soon lull you into a numbed state. If you can resist the urge to believe your next hand will be the complete one, you will find this pastime both relaxing and tiring.

Breathe sleepily

Have you ever noticed how relaxed a sleeping person's breathing sounds? Slow, deep, measured. You can use these same techniques to ease yourself into a relaxed, drowsy state.

Simply breathe deeply, concentrating on the bottom of your lungs rather than your chest; gradually slow down your breathing until the breaths become more and more leisurely; then listen closely your breath as it comes and goes.

Enjoy the silence

We live in an age when silence is often
considered a vacuum to be filled, or as an
absence rather than a gain.

The wonder of silence is that it is the first
step towards becoming calm and at peace —
something to be pursued and appreciated,
rather than avoided.

Regard silence this way, seek it in the
evening before bedtime, and you will rest
easier as the evening grows still.

Feel your tummy

When you really breathe deeply, your lower abdomen — not your chest and shoulders — swells with each breath.

If you can feel your tummy rise and fall this way, you're only a few breaths away from being deeply relaxed. Concentrate on breathing deeply, then breathing slowly, and you'll soon be ready to doze. (If not, you'll still enjoy a state of deep relaxation.)

Heal in the morning

Many medications, both pharmaceutical and herbal, initiate certain responses that interfere with your sleep. This can also apply to some vitamin supplements.

To remove this possible obstacle to your slumber, wherever possible take such medications in the morning or during the day.

Of course, this advice does not apply if taking them at night is part of the treatment.

Seek variety out of bed

Although different people need different amounts of sleep, those who follow the most disciplined sleeping routine usually claim to have the most satisfactory sleep. The same number of hours each night, every night, without variation.

If you feel your life needs variety, seek that variety in your waking hours — not in your sleeping hours. Routine improves sleep performance.

Spend yourself

Physical exhaustion is a sure course to sound sleep. Whether your exhaustion comes from intense exercise, dance, love-making, or a hard day at work, the results are the same — deep, satisfying sleep.

The converse of this is also true: while inactivity, sloth, and boredom may still produce tiredness, but they will not lead to a satisfying rest.

Roll over

The most relaxed sleeping position is not on your stomach, and probably not even on your side: it's on your back.

Providing you're not one to snore, sleep on your back and your body will rest more efficiently. Sleep on your back and your breathing will be deeper.

Waxing dreamily about wax

Far out! Something sleep-inducing, yet legal,
did come out of the Sixties.

The lava lamp.

While some may question its role in decor
aesthetics, the entrancing, changing shapes of
its rising and falling molten wax can have you
nodding off in no time.

Write out of worries

Even small worries have the capacity to hamper your sleep. One of the most efficient worry eliminators is the notebook.

If you find yourself with worries or problems before bedtime, jot them down in a notebook — then analyze the likelihood of their coming to pass, work them through, or postpone them until a specific time tomorrow.

Then go to bed with a clear mind.

Put beads in your bed

Over the centuries, worry beads, prayer beads, and prayer wheels have been used by millions of devoted users to dispense with nervous tension and to discover calm states.

Some say it's the repetitive action of the fingering, others say it's the stimulation of relaxing acupressure points in the hands. Either way, it is a simple, tangible way to drowsiness.

Cradle your finger

There are many well-rested people who swear
by the following getting-to-sleep ritual: lightly
grasp the forefinger of one hand in the palm
of the other, and cradle it until you doze off.
This is an Eastern energy-balancing technique
that capitalizes on the reflexology meridians
in the hand in order to help you relax.

Light up a joss stick

There is a property in smoldering incense that stimulates the production of serotonin, the neurochemical that helps you get to sleep.

While it may not be a good idea to burn anything in the bedroom itself, incense can have a powerfully relaxing effect in the hours leading to bedtime.

Reset the clock

Just half an hour's exposure to the morning sunlight is usually all it takes to reset your body clock after a long flight, nursing a new baby throughout the night, or any period of interrupted sleep.

Expose yourself to the sun in the morning, and you'll find it easier to sleep after the sun has set.

Pretend to be innocent

Deservedly, the innocent enjoy a soundness of sleep that the rest of us only fantasize about.

As you lie in bed, think back on a time of your own innocence — when your life was ruled by optimism and wonder, untempered by deadlines and responsibilities — and let your imagination re-experience those restful feelings tonight.

Indulge your body

There are few experiences in life that can relax, and put you in the mood for sleep, as effectively as a full body massage. The effects are equally as powerful be it Swedish, Shiatsu, Hawaiian, or Korean.

Treat yourself as often as you can afford. Justify it on the basis that it is as good for sleep as it is for the soul.

Formula for a beautiful sleep

A guaranteed formula for a beautiful sleep:
sleep in a beautiful bed, sleep under beautiful
bedclothes, wear beautiful nightwear,
and delight in it all under beautiful, soft
bedroom lights.

Try a different rhythm

The circadian rhythm for many people is not a strict twenty-four hours. If they were to live in a place with no clocks or sunlight (as experienced by underground cavers), some would sleep an hour longer each day.

You can take advantage of this circadian quirk to vary your own rhythm: go bed one hour later every night for week. After a week, you should be ready to fall asleep one hour earlier.

Forget norms

Please remember: if you have erratic sleep patterns, what you are experiencing is entirely normal. At any given time, a huge proportion of the population is sharing that same experience. Indeed, most people in the 40-50 age group have sleeping difficulties at some stage.

The good news is that, in most cases, it's temporary. And regular, restful sleep will come again.

Take a break by yourself

If you live in a crowded or noisy household,
you could profit by following this pre-bedroom
ritual: go to another room and devote half an
hour to yourself, alone with your thoughts,
without stimulation of any kind.

Take pleasure in your own company for
this time, and be surprised how readily
sleep follows.

Trim down

Excess body fat and restlessness often go hand in hand. As one of the first areas the body stores fat is at the base of the tongue, snoring and sleep apnea frequently accompany obesity.

Generally, the moment you begin to lose weight, you start to sleep better — some would find that a double incentive to watch their diet.

Train your bed

You can train yourself to associate your bed with restfulness rather than wakefulness by the practices you adopt.

Sleep-inducing beds permit only two activities: sleeping and sex. All other activities should be banished to other places — preferably other rooms.

Get the brush out

You can extract a dual benefit from brushing your hair, or having it brushed, before bedtime.

For a start, the gentle, repetitive effort is calming in its own right. More importantly, brushing stimulates many of the relaxing acupressure points in the scalp, which gives you a real head start on getting to sleep.

O sleep

O gentle sleep,
Nature's soft nurse! how have I frighted thee,
That thou no more wilt weigh my eyelids down
And steep my senses in forgetfulness?

—William Shakespeare
Henry IV

Clear the air

As houses can be traps for household dust, dust mites, animal hair, and other pollutants, an air purifier, or even an ionizer, can clear the way to a better sleep. An open window and regular vacuuming can have the same effect.

Keep your bedroom pollutant-free, especially denying your pets access. Before you know it, you'll be sleeping like a kitten.

Think about yawns

You've been conditioning yourself since childhood to associate yawning with sleep.

Ever noticed how you start yawning the moment someone else does? The same thing happens if you can imagine someone yawning: the clearer you can visualize this action, the more catching it becomes, and you start yawning yourself.

Turn away from the tube

While a book can be an ideal way to ease yourself into sleep mode, television often has the opposite effect. It is surprising how often you find the program that was sending you to sleep while you were watching it, will suddenly stimulate your thoughts the moment you go to bed.

Beware of the fizz

You knew colas were laced with caffeine. But
did you know that other, seemingly benign
soft drinks also had a caffeine content?
Some do. If you want to avoid restlessness,
avoid fizzy drinks at night.

Jet into bed

When you fly from one time zone to another, and jet lag becomes a risk, there is a simple procedure that will help you quickly adjust on arrival. Sleep for an hour or two after you land, then remain active until night. Next morning, you can adjust your body clock by allowing sunlight onto your skin at the first opportunity.

Revisit a fabulous moment

Add pleasure and beauty to those moments before sleep by reliving a beautiful experience.

Devote your full attention to it as you lie in bed. Visualize every detail. Try to recall every sound associated with it. Then try to recapture the feelings: what you felt, what the temperature was like, the tastes and textures.

What a fabulous way to drift off.

Talk up a dream

The words you use have a distinct effect on the thoughts and attitudes you have. This can be the difference between feeling positive or negative, happy or sad, tired or awake . . .

Talk yourself into tiredness by choosing words that relate to this sensation, repeating them until they take effect.

Try these: "I am feeling a great sense of peace and relief as I let go of the problems of the day, and gradually ease into a carefree, blissful sleep".

Look up to the clouds

Biofeedback experiments reveal that the
simple act of looking upwards, with unfocused
eyes, induces a restful state.

Make it even more restful by visualizing
a moving restful image. Imagine a small fluffy
cloud floating through a clear blue sky.
Imagine another following it. And another.
Slowly, methodically, repetitively.

In a way, it's like counting sheep.
Except it works.

Play the Saturday game

Notice how much easier it is to sleep on Friday or Saturday nights? There's no work tomorrow, the week's problems are behind you, and it doesn't matter if you oversleep a little in the morning.

Pretend it's Saturday tonight. Close your eyes and imagine waking up to a perfect day tomorrow. The sun will be shining, the birds chirping, and you rise to find a restful weekend still ahead of you.

Bathe at the end of the bed

A splendid little luxury almost totally over-looked in today's fast world is the footbath. Warm water, three or four drops of your favorite calming oil, a few rose petals, a fluffy white towel, and twenty minutes of bliss.

Do this at the foot of your bed so that you'll be ready for sleep before the sense of indulgence has passed.

Avoid puberty

The onset of puberty is usually accompanied
by a reduction in the secretion of melatonin,
the hormone that regulates your biorhythms
and helps make you sleepy. Bear this in mind
next time puberty approaches.

Turn the other way

Sometimes changing the lie of your bed can overcome persistent sleeplessness. Some say a North-South alignment aids sleep.

The nature of the Chinese art of *feng shui* is to align your living area with certain natural forces. This means your bed must never face the door, or be under an exposed beam. And mirrors, and furniture with sharp edges, must never face the bed.

What do you have to lose?

Howl at the moon

If you toss and turn on the night of full a moon, relax — millions of others are tossing and turning in exactly the same way.

Take care with chemicals

While prescription sedatives may sometimes
be useful, they should be treated with caution.
If you must use them, be aware that many
pharmaceutical sedatives will deny you a full
REM sleep, and may cause disrupted sleep
patterns for some time after you've stopped
using them.

Pass the sugar

A common cause of waking during the night is low blood sugar levels. You can easily prevent this from happening by taking a glass of warm milk or a light snack before you retire.

You might also consider that over-indulgence in sugar during the day can contribute to lowered blood sugar levels at night.

Sleep like a baby

When you have a new baby in the house, sleep deprivation becomes a matter of course.

To add a semblance of regular sleep to your schedule, here is one practice well worth adopting: learn to sleep when baby sleeps (up to eighteen hours a day).

While those brief snatches may feel unsatisfying, in the long run they will help you feel more rested.

Think of Caesar

In Julius Caesar's time, the popular treatment for insomnia was an infusion made from the flower of the bitter orange tree. Today, this same ingredient is readily available in the form of the essential oil, neroli.

Add a few drops to your bath water. Sprinkle a drop on your pillow case. And doze off with pleasant memories of a distant age.

Take care of your day

The attitudes and activities that make up your day invariably impact on the way you sleep at night. Concentrate on making your day as fulfilling and harmonious as possible, perform every daytime action to the best of your ability, and you'll find it easier to enjoy trouble-free sleep at night.

Point at your wrist

There is a powerful relaxing acupressure
point at the crease of your wrist directly up
from your ring finger — you will feel a small,
sensitive indentation at this place.

By applying a firm downward pressure with
your forefinger as you breathe out, then
releasing the pressure as you breathe in,
you will ease yourself into a calmer and
calmer state.

Take your time

You'll feel better about your sleeping routine, just by applying a little patience.

Long-term sleep problems are not always solved overnight. Take your time finding a solution. Strive for little improvements. As long as the improvement trend line is positive, you're heading in the right direction.

Get ready for bed before sunset

The moment your head hits the pillow is not time to start shedding your thoughts of the day, and making your preparations for tomorrow.

Better to start preparing for sleep earlier in the afternoon, either working through the issues of the day or postponing them. Then, when night falls, you can concentrate your attention on getting the most out of your rest.

Give up your diet

How long have you been searching for the perfect excuse to abandon that radical diet? Here it is: dieting often has an adverse effect on the quality of your sleep. A sensible, well-balanced diet is the first step to a sensible, well-balanced sleep.

Fill your mind with nothing

One of the hindrances to a sound sleep is the restlessness of thought. By its very nature, thought is restless, constantly moving from one concept to another.

Thoughts can be quelled simply by filling the mind with something else. Concentrate on the sound of your breathing. Or, if you know a mantra meditation, concentrate on the sound of your mantra. Soon there will be no room for thought. And when there is no room for thought, sleep comes.

Poke your tongue

Stress has a habit of encouraging two conditions, often interlinked: disturbed sleep and tightened jaw muscles. When your jaw muscles are clenched and you grind your teeth, tension begins to spread to other parts of your body. Before you know it, your sleep is disturbed.

You can overcome this by lightly pressing your tongue against the roof of your mouth. It will relax your jaw muscles, and add a smile to your sleep.

Choose your bed partners well

Don't tell the person beside you that I said this, but one of the most common causes of sleep disturbance is not your attitude or your physiology.

It is your partner.

If you sleep with someone who is noisy or restless, consider one of the following: wear earplugs, get twin beds, or, in extreme cases, have separate rooms.

Breathe yourself awake

How do you stay awake the day after a
sleepless night?

Many think coffee is the answer — but it
can disrupt the *next* night's sleep.

A better way of staying awake is to use a
yoga technique known as circular breathing.
Cover one nostril, breathe in. Cover the other
nostril, breathe out. Breathe in through the
same nostril. Cover that one and breathe out.
Continue until you are wide awake.

Remember Grandma

Remember what grandmother used to say
about retiring early? "An hour before midnight
is worth two after."

Who am I to argue with Grandma?

About the author

Paul Wilson is known the world over as the "guru of calm". His first book, *The Calm Technique*, is considered one of the most influential in the genre. His second, *Instant Calm*, was a giant bestseller, and was translated into eighteen languages. The success continued with *Calm at Work*, *The Little Book of Calm at Work*, and *The Little Book of Pleasure*.

However, the one that won the greatest acclaim is *The Little Book of Calm*. With sales of over 3,000,000 it has spent more than 2 years at the top of the bestseller lists. Now, with *The Little Book of Sleep*, the peace begins to spread in a slightly new direction.

Feel free to contact the author or share your calm at
http://www.calmcentre.com